The Nature Kid's Guide to
SKUNKS

DAVID ANDERSON

LP Media Inc. Publishing
Text copyright © 2026 by LP Media Inc.
All rights reserved.

For information address LP Media Inc. Publishing,
30012 Variolite St NW, Princeton MN 55371
www.lpmedia.org

Publication Data

Skunks
The Nature Kid's Guide to Skunks — First edition.

Summary: "Learn all about Skunks, the Nature Kid Way"
— Provided by publisher.

ISBN: 979-8-89818-168-0

[1. Skunks – Non-Fiction] I. Title.

Title: The Nature Kid's Guide to Skunks

CONTENTS

SNEAKY STRIPES

Skunks can dig their own dens, but they often use burrows that were abandoned by other animals.

Scurry! A fluffy skunk sneaks behind a big rock. It wiggles its nose.

Skunks live in many different places. They like forests with lots of brush, and grasslands work well too. Both places give them cover to stay safe.

Skunks need places to hide and dig. They like areas with soft, loose soil. This helps them make dens underground.

Skunks also live near people now. Yards and parks have good hiding spots. Woodpiles and porches make cozy dens. Skunks find food in these places too.

Skunks can handle different weather. They stay active in both warm and cool temperatures.

SKUNK SPOTS

Whoosh! A breeze carries the scent of a spotted skunk.

Skunks live across North America. They are found from Canada to Mexico.

The striped skunk is the most common skunk in North America. You can find them in every state! Spotted skunks are smaller and harder to find. They live in parts of the west, central, and southeastern United States.

Skunks usually only travel about 1 to 2 miles from their dens. They stay in one area all year.

Spotted skunks do a handstand before they spray! They flip up onto their front legs, walk toward the predator, and then let it rip!

SMALL STINKERS

Pitter-patter! A striped skunk walks through the brush.

Skunks are small animals. Most striped skunks weigh only 3 to 12 pounds. They are roughly the size of a house cat.

They grow to be 13 to 18 inches long. Their fluffy tails add 7 to 10 more inches.

A striped skunk stands only about 6 inches tall.

Spotted skunks are even tinier. They can weigh less than a pound, making them no bigger than a squirrel!

Baby skunks are about the size of a mouse when they are born. They fit in a teaspoon!

BLACK AND
WHITE
10

A striped skunk lifts its fluffy tail in warning. Watch out!

Skunks have stout bodies with short legs. Their fur is black with white markings. These bold colors warn other animals to stay away.

Spotted skunks have broken stripes and spots. This pattern looks different from solid stripes. Their fur is also soft and thick.

Skunks have sharp claws on their front paws. These claws help them dig for food. Their back feet have shorter claws for walking.

Skunk teeth are very sharp. They have 34 teeth for crunching bugs and other food!

SNIFF IT

Sniff! A striped skunk walks across a gravel path. He's searching for a meal!

Skunks have an amazing sense of smell. Their noses can find bugs hiding underground. They smell food that people cannot smell at all.

But skunks do not see very well. They can only see things that are close by.

Their ears help make up for weak eyes. They can hear soft sounds in the dark.

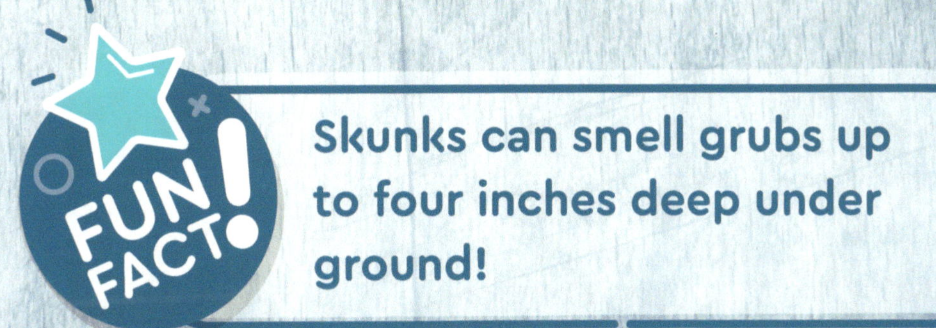

STINKY SPRAY

Splash! The skunk's spray fills the night air. Watch out!

Skunks have a powerful way to stay safe. They spray a stinky liquid from glands near their tail. This smell can reach up to a mile away!

The spray burns if it gets in eyes. This makes predators run away fast. Most animals learn to leave skunks alone.

Spotted skunks do a handstand before they spray. This pose warns enemies to back off.

Skunk spray is made of oily chemicals called thiols. The smell can last for days!

MUNCH TIME

Chomp! Little teeth tear into a juicy berry. Time for dinner!

Skunks eat many different foods. They are **omnivores**, which means they eat both plants and animals.

Skunks love to eat insects. They munch on beetles, crickets, and grasshoppers. **Grubs** are a favorite treat.

Skunks also eat fruits and berries. They snack on mice, eggs, and worms too. In summer, one skunk can eat hundreds of bugs each night!

Skunks eat bees! When they catch one, they roll it on the ground to rub off the stinger. Then they gobble it up sting-free!

DIG IN

A single skunk can dig up over 100 small holes in one night while searching for grubs and insects!

Dig! Dirt flies as a spotted skunk hunts for bugs in the yard.

Skunks use their strong sense of smell to find hidden food. Once they smell it they use their long claws to dig in soil. These sharp nails break through hard ground easily.

Spotted skunks often search for food in rocky areas. They squeeze into small spaces between rocks. Their slim bodies help them reach bugs in tight spots.

Skunks sniff the ground as they walk. When they smell something tasty, they start digging right away. They push dirt aside with their front paws. Sometimes they roll over logs to find grubs underneath.

WATCH OUT

Trot! A skunk walks through the grass, it's ears listen for danger.

Skunks have many enemies in the wild. Great horned owls are their main **predator**. These owls cannot smell well, so the skunk's stinky spray does not bother them!

Coyotes and foxes sometimes hunt skunks too. But they learn quickly. Predators usually stay away after getting sprayed once.

Bobcats may try to catch young skunks. Cars are very dangerous. Many skunks get hit crossing roads at night.

A skunk's spray does not just smell bad. It can sting a predator's eyes and even cause temporary blindness.

STOMP AND SPRAY

Run! A skunk lifts its tail and sprays a stinky cloud.

Skunks have clever ways to stay safe. When scared, they stomp their front feet hard. This warns enemies to back off.

Spotted skunks do something amazing. They do a handstand! This makes them look bigger and scarier.

If stomping does not work, skunks spray. They can aim up to 10 feet away. Most animals run before the stink comes!

Skunk spray contains sulfur chemicals like those found in onions and garlic.

WADDLE WALK

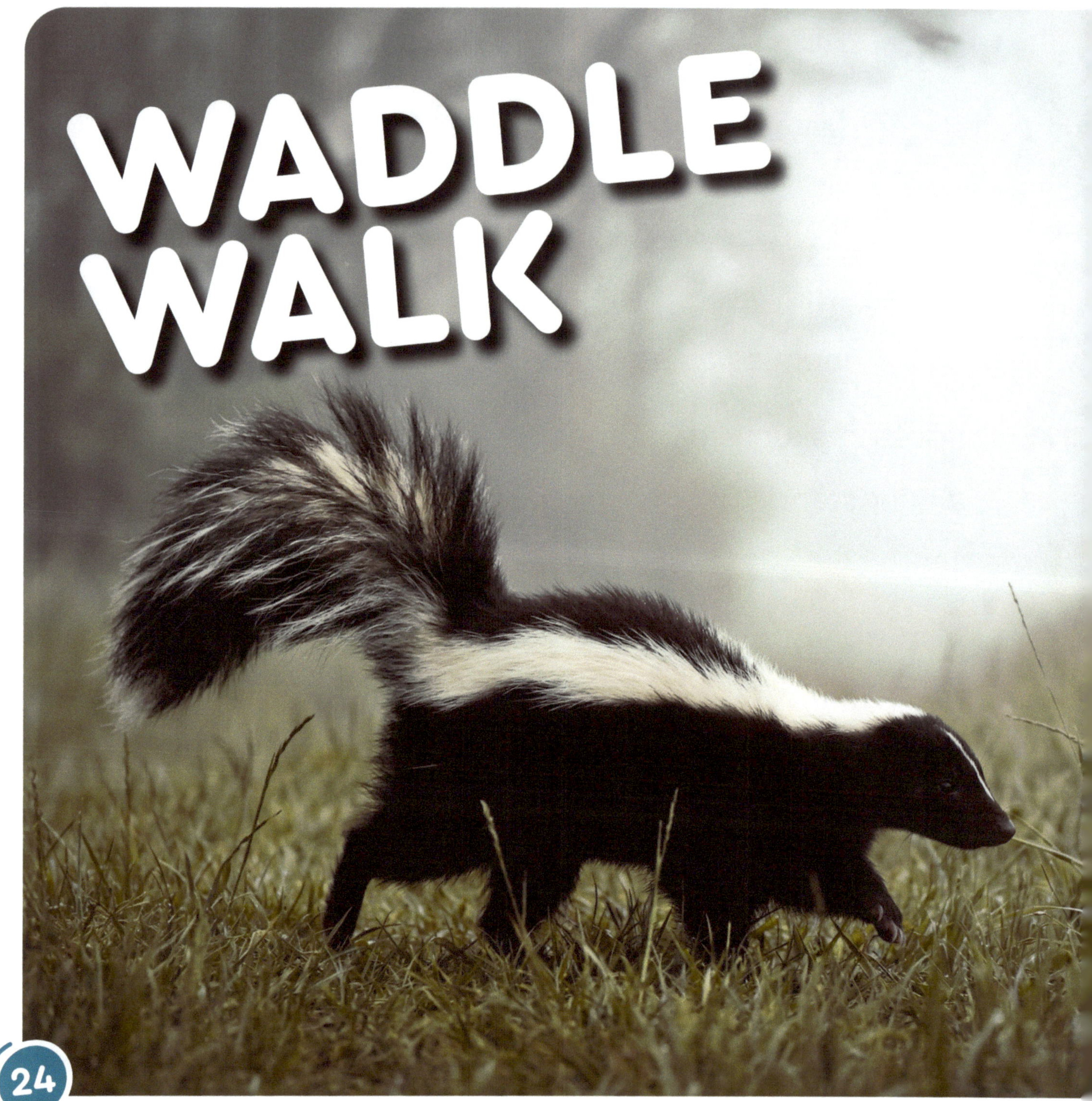

Scamper! A fluffy skunk waddles through an open field.

Skunks are slow movers. They waddle when they walk. Their short legs take many small steps.

Striped skunks cannot run fast. They only reach 10 miles per hour. This is slower than most predators.

Spotted skunks are good climbers. They use their claws to climb trees. Some skunks can also swim across small streams.

Spotted skunks are much quicker than striped skunks. They can dart, dodge, and even climb straight up a tree trunk in seconds!

NIGHT PROWLERS

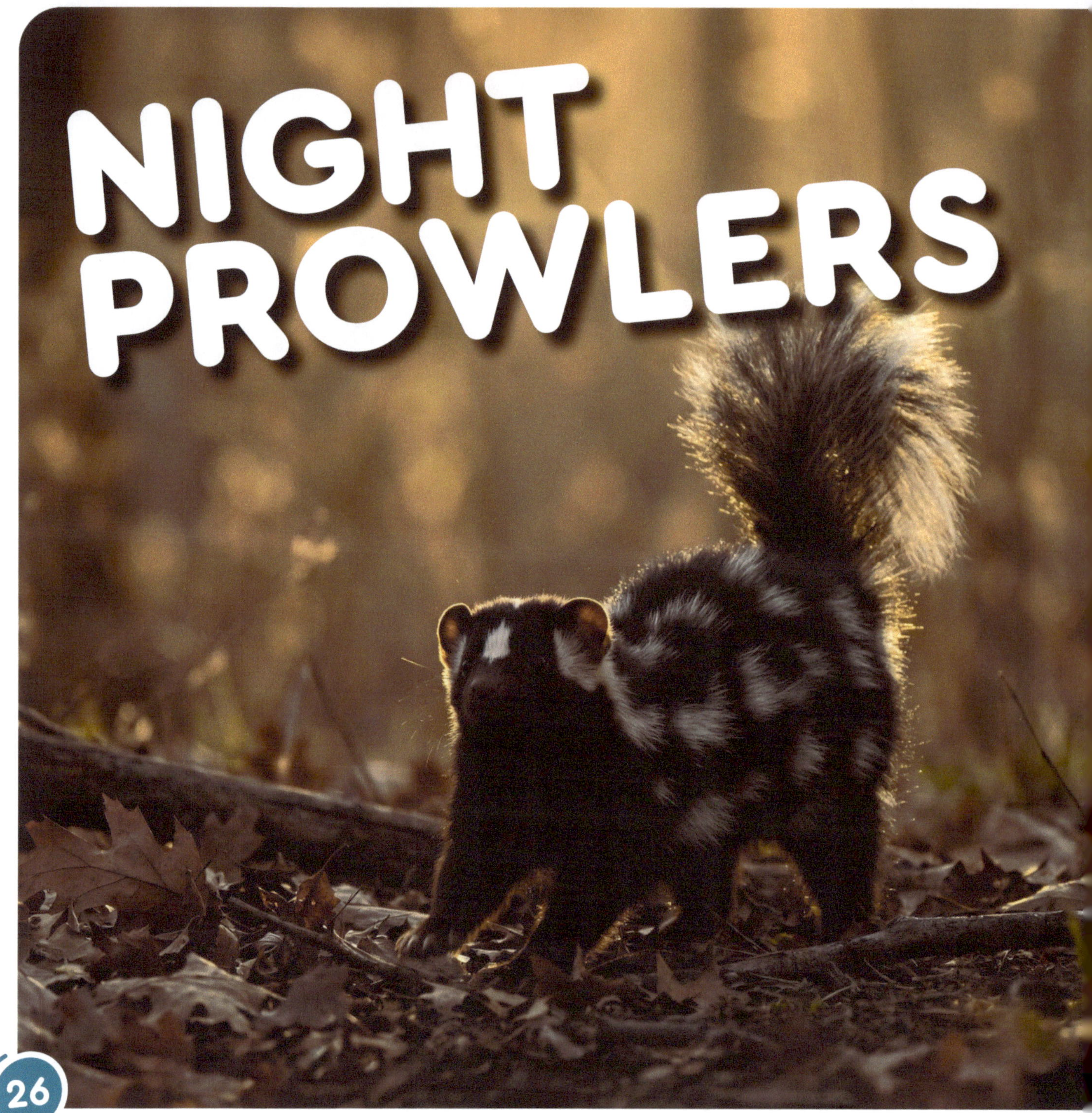

Squeak! The moon rises and a spotted skunk leaves it's den.

Skunks are **nocturnal** animals. They sleep during the day and come out at night. Darkness helps keep them safe from predators.

Spotted skunks rest in dens during daylight. They hide in hollow logs, rock piles, or old burrows. When night falls, they leave to find food.

Skunks spend their nights searching for meals. They sniff the ground and dig for bugs. By sunrise, they return home.

A skunk's eyes reflect light in the dark, just like a cat's eyes.

LIVING SOLO

Rustle! A lone skunk waddles through the quiet woods.

Most skunks live alone. They do not form packs or herds. Each skunk finds food by itself.

Striped skunks usually stay apart. But they meet to mate in spring.

In cold winter months, skunks share dens for warmth. Up to 12 females may sleep together. Males usually den alone. Even when they share dens, there is no leader.

Skunks may groom each other during mating season. They lick and nibble each other's fur.

MATING SEASON

Chirp! Two skunks waddle through moonlit flowers. They will be mates.

Skunks mate in late winter and early spring. This makes February and March busy months for these animals.

Male skunks can smell females from far away. They follow these scent trails to find mates. Several males may visit the same female.

Male skunks stomp their feet and make noises to get attention. Spotted skunks also do a special dance to impress females.

Mother skunks are pregnant for about 66 days. Baby skunks are called kits.

CUTE KITS

Snuggle! Fuzzy skunk babies wiggle in their cozy den.

Baby skunks are born in spring, usually in April or May. A mother skunk has 4 to 7 kits at once.

Newborn kits are very small, weighing less than one ounce each. That is lighter than a slice of bread!

Kits are born with their eyes closed. They cannot see for about three weeks. But their black and white stripes show right away, even on their pink skin.

Skunk kits can spray when they are only eight days old!

33

MOM KNOWS BEST

Mother skunks can move their whole litter to a new den in one night.

Whoosh! A striped skunk guides her babies through tall grass.

Mother skunks raise their babies alone. Fathers do not help at all. Mom finds food, keeps kits safe, and teaches them everything.

Kits drink their mother's milk for about two months. Then mom teaches them to find food. She shows them how to dig for bugs and grubs.

Young skunks follow their mother in a single file line. They also learn how to use their spray by practicing.

After about three months, kits leave to live on their own.

SUPER SURVIVORS

Skunks can survive snake bites that would kill other animals. They even eat venomous snakes! Their bodies have special defenses against venom.

Swoosh! A striped skunk waddles through tall grass.

Skunks have lived on Earth for millions of years. They even survived the Ice Age!

As the world changed around them, skunks adapted. When forests were cut down for farms, skunks moved right in. When towns and cities grew, skunks found new hiding spots under buildings and porches.

Scientists believe skunks have survived so long because of two things. Their spray scares away almost every predator. And they will eat almost anything, so they never run out of food.

FUN FACT!

Skunks spray only as a last resort. They have enough spray for five or six shots.

Look! A striped skunk waddles through a backyard garden.

Want to spot a skunk? You might not have to go far. Skunks love neighborhoods with gardens, sheds, and big trees.

The best time to look is right after sunset. Bring a flashlight and walk slowly along fences and garden edges. Look for two small glowing eyes low to the ground.

During the day, check your yard for small holes in the grass. That is a sign a skunk visited during the night. If you find one, always watch from far away!

GLOSSARY

dens
Underground homes where animals sleep and stay safe.

omnivores
Animals that eat both plants and other animals.

predators
Animals that hunt and eat other animals.

nocturnal
Awake at night and asleep during the day.

grubs
Baby bugs that live in the dirt.

www.ingramcontent.com/pod-product-compliance
Lightning Source LLC
Chambersburg PA
CBHW041620110726
48005CB00002B/453